WHSmith

Challenge
Science
KS2: Year 3
Age 7–8

Lynn Huggins-Cooper

Text and illustrations © Hodder Education

First published in 2007
exclusively for WHSmith by
Hodder Education,
part of Hachette Livre UK,
338 Euston Road
London NW1 3BH

Impression number   10 9 8 7 6 5 4 3
Year   2010

Cover illustration by Sally Newton Illustrations

Typeset by Servis Filmsetting Ltd, Manchester

Printed and bound in Spain

A CIP record for this book is available from the
British Library

ISBN: 978 0 340 94550 6

Contents

Parents' notes

How this book can help your child

- This book has been written for children who are 7–8 years old.
- It will support and improve the work they are doing at school, whichever Science course they use.
- The activities in the book have been carefully written to include the knowledge expected of children at this stage in their development.

Using this book

- There are 24 topics and 4 tests in the book. A test occurs after 6 topics have been completed.
- Each topic need not be completed in one session. Think of it as about a week's work.
- Try to supplement "paper" activities with safe, hands-on Science activities: use cooking as an opportunity to look at changes of state and reversible/irreversible change; spend time in the garden looking at plant and animal diversity, etc.
- Do give help and encouragement. Completing the activities should not become a chore.
- Do let your child mark his or her own work under your supervision and correct any careless mistakes he or she might have made.
- When all the tests have been completed let your child fill in the Certificate of Achievement on the opposite page.
- Each double page has a title, explanation of the learning point, practice section, and challenge section.

Topic – the main learning point

Get started – helpful information and tips about the learning point

Practice – straightforward follow-up to the learning point

Challenge – uses the learning point in a slightly different way and takes it further

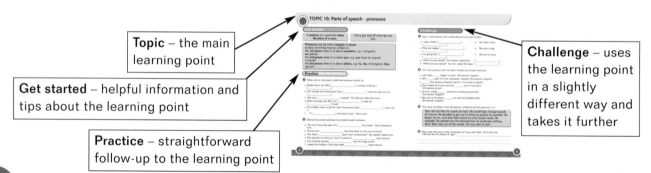

This certifies
that

_____

has completed

CHALLENGE SCIENCE YEAR 3

on _____

Scoring _____ on TEST 1

_____ on TEST 2

_____ on TEST 3

and _____ on TEST 4

**Total score
out of 80** _____

40–50	good effort
50–60	well done
60–70	fantastic
70–80	brilliant

Topic 1: What do plants need to grow?

Green plants need **water**, **light** and the **right temperature** to grow. If you put a green plant in the dark for a few days, it soon turns yellow. If you do not give a plant enough water, it will soon wilt and then go brown and dry up.

Practice

1 **True or false? Put T or F in the boxes.**

a Plants need water and sleep to grow. . . . . □

b Plants need light and water to grow. . . . . □

c Plants can turn yellow if they are put in the dark. . . . . □

d Plants can turn pink if they are put in a dark place. . . . . □

e Plants can dry up and go brown if they do not have
enough water. . . . . □

f Plants can dry up if they do not have enough light. . . . . □

Challenge

2 Answer these by underlining the correct response.

a Imagine you are growing some daisies in a pot. Where would you put the plant pot?

   i in a cupboard

   ii under the bed

   iii on the windowsill

   iv in the fridge

b Your plant is looking dry and brown. What has happened?

   i You have put it somewhere dark.

   ii You have not given it enough water, so it has dried out.

   iii You have given it too much water, so it has dried out.

c Where could you put a plant with sickly yellow leaves to make them go green again?

   i under the sink

   ii in a cupboard

   iii on a windowsill

3 Match the plant to the description.

a yellow leaves		i plant with enough light and water
b green leaves		ii plant without enough light
c dry brown leaves		iii plant without enough water

Topic 2: Plants from seeds

Get started

Have you ever looked at a tiny seed and wondered how a huge tree can grow from it?

There are lots of different types of seeds. Look in the garden or in the park in the autumn and you will be amazed at how many you find!

Some seeds, like sycamore "helicopters", acorns and conkers, will grow into new trees if you plant them. Other seeds, like beans and peas, will grow into food plants.

When a seed is starting to grow, we say it has **germinated**.

Seeds need water and the right temperature to germinate.

Some seeds need light, too.

Practice

1 **True or false? Put T or F in the boxes.**

a Lots of plants grow from seeds. . . . . □

b Sycamore "helicopters" that fall from the trees are seeds. . . . . □

c The peas we eat with our dinner are seeds. . . . . □

d If you plant petals, they will grow. . . . . □

e Plants do not grow from seeds. . . . . □

Challenge

2 **Fill in the missing words using the words in the box.**

| seeds | germinated | trees | light | temperature |

a When a seed starts to grow, we say it has _____.

b Plants grow from tiny _____.

c Seeds need water and the right _____ to germinate (start to grow).

d Sycamore helicopters, acorns and conkers will all grow into new _____ if you plant them.

e Some, but not all, seeds need _____ to start to grow.

3 **Using the things in the box, write instructions in four steps for planting seeds.**

a First, I would _____

_____.

b Then I would _____

_____.

c Next, I would _____

_____.

d Lastly, I would _____

_____.

Topic 3: Parts of a plant

When we say we like "flowers", we usually mean the whole plant! If you look at a "bunch" of flowers, you will find it usually contains stems and leaves as well as petals.

All of the different parts of a plant have a **function** (a job to do). The **flower** can have bright **petals** and smell nice, and this makes insects visit. Some plants need insects to move pollen from one plant to another. The **leaf** uses sunlight to make food for the plant. The **stem** is like a straw that takes water and goodness to different parts of the plant. The **roots** hold the plant steady in the ground, and take up water and nutrients from the soil.

Practice

1 Label the parts of this flowering plant.

Challenge

2 **Fill in the missing words. The words you need are in the flower shapes.**

 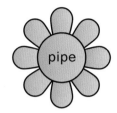  

a The _____ hold the plant in the soil.

b Leaves make _____ using sunlight.

c The stem of a plant is like a _____ that takes water from the roots to the other parts of the plant.

d _____ are sometimes brightly coloured so that insects will visit the plant.

3 **Match the part of the plant to the job it does.**

| a stem | | i holds the plant in the ground |

| b leaf | | ii makes food using sunlight |

| c petal | | iii takes water and nutrients from the roots to the other parts of the plant |

| d root | | iv smells nice and is a bright colour to attract insects |

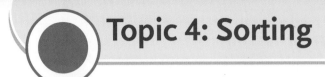

Topic 4: Sorting

You can sort living things into groups by looking at similarities and differences – what is the same and what is different about them.

A dog, a crab, a whelk and a seal could be sorted into groups in the following ways:

crab, whelk: have a shell
dog, seal: do not have a shell

or

dog: does not live in or near the sea
crab, whelk, seal: live in or near the sea

Practice

1. **Sort these creatures into the correct part of the table.**

frog	grasshopper	butterfly	great diving beetle

lives in a pond	does not live in a pond

Challenge

2 Sort these creatures into the two boxes.

| ladybird | grasshopper | butterfly | blackbird |

| **is an insect** |
| |

| **is not an insect** |
| |

How else could you sort the creatures into two groups? _____

_____

3 Use this Venn diagram to sort these creatures into groups.

| otter | cat | fish | crocodile |

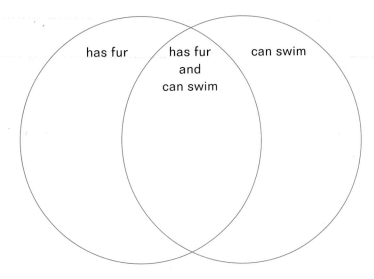

has fur   has fur
                 and
                 can swim   can swim

Which creature is a member of both groups, or sets? _____

Topic 5: The seven life processes

All living things do certain things – that is how we know they are alive!

All living things:

- move
- grow and change
- reproduce (produce babies)
- breathe
- feel things
- feed
- get rid of waste.

Careful, though – sometimes it is hard to see all these things happening! Plants do not breathe in the same way as humans, but they do take in and give out gases. We cannot usually see plants moving, either – but they do grow towards the light.

Practice

1 **Match the two parts of the sentences together so they make sense.**

a Living things grow

b Even plants

c If something is alive

d Living things have to

e If something gets rid of waste

f A plant is

i it produces young (babies).

ii move, like all living things.

iii it is alive.

iv a living thing.

v feed to stay alive.

vi and change.

Challenge

2 **Draw a circle round the things that are alive.**

a fish   e baby   i starfish

     b tree   f pen

c rock   g rabbit   j plate

     d sunflower   h seaweed

3 **Write the names of six living things in the leaf and six things that are not living in the rock.**

Topic 6: Alive or never alive?

In the last topic we saw how we can tell that things are alive.

Now we are going to check if we can tell what **is** alive, what was **once** alive, and what has **never** been alive!

Practice

1 Sort these things into the correct part of the table.

waves   bird   fire   plant growing in pot   dried grass   tree   stone   carrot

alive	once alive	never alive

Challenge

2 Draw two things that are alive and two things that have never been alive.

Alive	Never alive

3 Circle the things in the word wall that have never been alive.

stone	plastic doll	dried grass	log of wood
	fox	lettuce	ladybird	
metal spoon	polystyrene cup	ceramic plate	oak tree

Test 1

Topic 1

1 What would a plant look like if it had been left to grow in the dark for two weeks? (1 mark)

_____

2 What would happen to a plant that was not given enough water? (1 mark)

_____

Topic 2

3 What do we mean when we say a seed has "germinated"? (1 mark)

_____

Topic 3

4 Match the part of the plant to what it does. (3 marks)

a leaf	i attracts insects with its scent and colour
b root	ii holds the plant in the ground
c petal	iii makes food using sunlight

Topic 4

5 Sort the creatures in the box into the correct part of the table. (2 marks)

| cat | horse | newt | frog |
| badger | tadpole | butterfly | crab |

lives in or near water	lives on land

6 How else could you sort these animals into groups? (1 mark)

_____

Topic 5

7 True or false? Put T or F in the boxes. (4 marks)

a Trees are not alive. . . . . ☐

b All living things reproduce. . . . . ☐

c Not all living things get rid of waste. . . . . ☐

d All living things move. . . . . ☐

Topic 6

8 Alive or never alive? Write A for Alive or N for Never alive in the boxes. (2 marks)

a pen ☐   b caterpillar ☐   c dog ☐   d tree ☐   e crab ☐

f pebble ☐   g computer ☐   h crayon ☐   i raindrop ☐   j sunlight ☐

9 Circle the things in the word wall that have never been alive. (4 marks)

stone	plastic ruler	onion	dried grass	
	china doll	ladybird	metal spoon	lion

Mark the test. Remember to fill in your score on page 3.

Write your score out of 19.   ☐

Add a bonus point if you scored 15 or more.

TOTAL SCORE FOR TEST 1   ☐

Topic 7: Habitats

Get started

A **habitat** is the place where something lives. A garden is a habitat, and so is the seashore or the woods. You find creatures in one habitat that you may not find in another.

Practice

1 **Who lives where? Match each creature to its habitat.**

a crab

b hedgehog

c owl

d tadpole

e woodlouse

f shark

g spider

h pike

i seashore

ii woodland

iii pond

iv garden

v house

vi lake

vii rotting log

viii ocean

Challenge

2 **Fill in the missing letters to find the hidden habitats.**

a p__n__

b se__s__ore

c __ard__n

d w__ __dlan__

e hedge__ __w

3 **Draw a creature that lives in each habitat.**

woodland	pond

seashore	garden

Topic 8: Caring for the environment

It is very important that we care for the **environment** – the world around us. If we do not want to spoil or harm the environment, we need to look after it. Litter looks horrible and can harm animals. Creatures such as mice can crawl into bottles and then cannot climb out again, and birds can get tangled in string, nets and plastic. Rubbish should always be disposed of carefully. Some can be **recycled**.

Practice

1. **Paper, cans and glass can be recycled. Put the rubbish into the correct recycling bin. Draw arrows.**

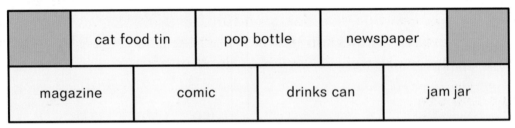

	cat food tin	pop bottle	newspaper	
magazine	comic		drinks can	jam jar

GLASS

CANS

PAPER

Challenge

2 We can re-use or recycle things so that there is less rubbish. Match the rubbish to what it could be used for.

a scraps of material from old clothes	**i** doll's house
b ice cream tub	**ii** container for small toys
c big cardboard box	**iii** pencil pot
d yoghurt pot	**iv** patchwork quilt

3 Design a rubbish bin! Using the materials below, and any other "rubbish" you can think of, design a rubbish bin that you could make for your bedroom. You could make a monster or a huge frog with an open mouth, for example. Draw your dustbin here.

> **You could use . . .**
>
> cardboard boxes
>
> egg cartons
>
> cardboard tubes
>
> bubble wrap plastic
>
> plastic tubs
>
> . . . and so on!

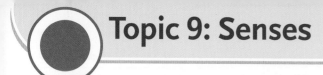

Topic 9: Senses

We can explore the world around us using our five senses:

| smell | taste | sight | hearing | touch |

Practice

1. **Label this boy to show which sense goes with which part of his body.**
   Use the words smell, taste, see, hear and touch.

Challenge

2 **Finish these sentences.**

| tongue | fingers | ears | eyes | nose |

a I smell things with my _____.

b I see things with my _____.

c I hear things with my _____.

d I taste things with my _____.

e I feel things with all of my skin, and I touch things with my _____.

3 **Which sense did I use? Finish these sentences.**

a I felt my cat's fur with my fingers.
I used _____.

b My nose "told" me my dinner would be delicious!
I used _____.

c That sherbet was really sour!
I used _____.

d I looked at an interesting green beetle.
I used _____.

e I heard a loud "BANG"!
I used _____.

Topic 10: Teeth

We use our teeth to eat food. Without them, we would not be able to chew and bite our food.

Cleaning our teeth helps to remove pieces of food left behind after we eat. If we do not clean our teeth, the **bacteria** in our mouths breaks the pieces of food down into sugars. The sugars make a sticky coating on our teeth, which is called **plaque**. The plaque can cause tooth decay.

Practice

1 **Fill in the missing words to complete the sentences.**

clean	bacteria	decay	food	chewing	plaque

a We use our teeth for _____ our food.

b It is very important that we _____ our teeth every day.

c We clean our teeth to brush away bits of _____ that may be left behind.

d _____ in our mouths break food down into sugars.

e _____ is sticky and can harm our teeth if we do not brush it away.

f If we do not brush away plaque, our teeth can _____. This means they go bad.

Challenge

2 **True or false? Put T or F in the boxes.**

a Eating too many sticky sweets is good for our teeth. . . . . ☐

b Plaque is sticky and we need to brush it away. . . . . ☐

c We should never brush our teeth, in case we wear them away. . . . . . . ☐

d We need to brush our teeth twice every day. . . . . ☐

e Brushing regularly causes tooth decay. . . . . ☐

f We should visit the dentist every six months. . . . . ☐

3 **Design a poster to help people to keep their teeth healthy. Think about the things they should and should not do, and include them in your poster. Draw a picture of two things people should do under the big tick, and two things people should not do under the cross.**

✓   ✗

Topic 11: Food groups

We need to eat lots of different sorts of food to get all the goodness we need to grow and stay healthy: **protein**, **fats**, **carbohydrates** and **vitamins**.

Fibre and **water** also help us to digest our food and keep us healthy.

- Fresh vegetables and fruit contain fibre and lots of vitamins.
- Butter and cooking oils are fats. These give us lots of energy and can be stored by the body to use later.
- Pasta, cereal and bread contain carbohydrates, which give us energy.
- Cheese, meat, milk and nuts contain lots of protein, which helps our bodies to grow and repair themselves.

Practice

1 **Circle the healthiest option from each set.**

a	banana	cake	biscuit
b	toffee	wholemeal bread	ice lolly
c	pasta	jelly	ice cream
d	cola	milk	lemonade
e	orange mousse	orange cake	orange
f	apple juice	apple pie	apple tart

Challenge

2 **Match the food to the food group. Draw a line from the food to the correct group.**

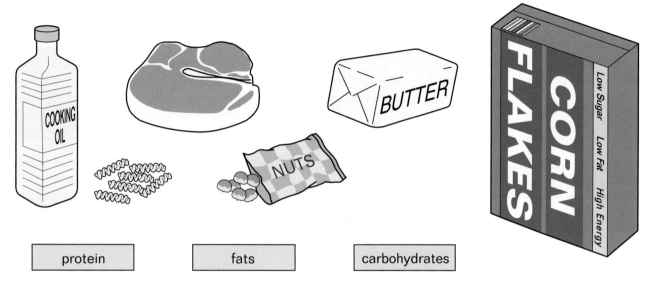

| protein | fats | carbohydrates |

3 **Use the clues to fill in the crossword.**

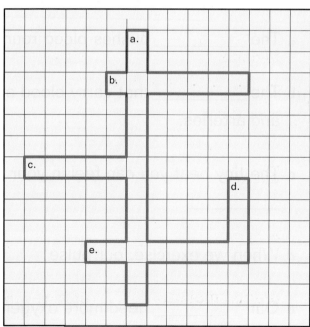

Across

b cheese and milk contain this

c carbohydrates and fats are a good source of this, which lets us run and play

e fresh fruit and vegetables contain many of these

Down

a pasta, cereal and bread are a good source of this food group

d cooking oil and butter are a source of this food group

Topic 12: The heart and exercise

The **heart** pushes (pumps) blood round the body. It uses tubes called **veins** and **arteries** to move the blood to all parts of the body.

When we take exercise, our heart pumps faster. This is to get more oxygen, dissolved in the blood, to our muscles. They need more oxygen when they are working hard. As we start to breathe faster, our heart works harder to move the blood round the body quickly. This makes the **pulse**, the tiny beat you can feel in your wrist and neck, beat faster (or "rise").

Practice

1 Fill in the missing words to complete the sentences.

| pulse | heart | muscles | rises | tubes |

a The _____ pushes blood round the body.

b The _____ that carry blood around our bodies are called veins and arteries.

c The tiny beat you can feel in your neck and wrist is called your _____.

d When we exercise, our pulse _____.

e Our _____ need more oxygen when they are working hard.

Challenge

2 **True or false? Put** T **or** F **in the boxes.**

a The lungs push blood around the body. . . . . ☐

b Veins and arteries are the tubes that move blood around
the body. . . . . ☐

c When we exercise, our hearts beat faster because we are
hungry. . . . . ☐

d The beat you can feel in your wrist and neck is called your
pump. . . . . ☐

e The beat you can feel in your wrist and neck is called your
pulse. . . . . ☐

f Our bodies need more blood when our muscles are working
hard. . . . . ☐

3 **Fill in the missing letters in these words from this topic.**

a pu__se

b ex__ __ci__e

c he__ __t

d v__i__s

e art__ __ies

4 **Name four types of exercise that would make your heart beat faster.**

a _____

b _____

c _____

d _____

Test 2

Topic 7

1 Who lives where? Match the animal to its habitat. (4 marks)

a owl	i Arctic
b jellyfish	ii woodland
c camel	iii sea
d polar bear	iv desert

Topic 8

2 The items in the box are ready to be thrown away.

glass lemonade bottle	jam jar	comic
pickle jar	bean tin	plastic milk bottle
plastic egg box	newspaper	lemonade can
cardboard cereal box	magazine	cat food tin

a Name the items that could be put in a bottle bank. (1 mark) _____

_____

b Name the items that could be put in a newspaper recycling bin. (1 mark)

_____

c Name the items that could be put in a can bank. (1 mark) _____

_____

Topic 9

3 Name our five senses. (5 marks) _____ _____

_____ _____ _____

Topic 10

4 Why should we brush our teeth? (2 marks) _____

_____

_____

Topic 11

5 Which snack in each pair will give you more vitamins? (3 marks)

a apple ☐ **or** biscuit ☐

b fresh orange juice ☐ **or** fizzy orange ☐

c crisps ☐ **or** carrot sticks ☐

Topic 12

6 Circle the correct words in the brackets to complete the sentences.
(2 marks)

a Our bodies need (less/more) oxygen when our muscles are working
hard.

b The tiny beat you can feel in your neck and wrist is called your
(pulse/pump).

Mark the test. Remember to fill in your score on page 3.

Write your score out of 19. ☐

Add a bonus point if you scored 15 or more.

TOTAL SCORE FOR TEST 2 ☐

Topic 13: Animal life cycles

Get started

Have you noticed how things change as they grow? Some creatures just seem to get bigger, with the **young** (babies) looking like small **adults** (grown-ups). Other creatures change completely as they grow. A tadpole, for example, looks nothing like a frog.

Practice

1 Match the "young" (baby) animals to the adult animals by drawing a line between them.

a tadpole

b caterpillar

i cat

ii hen

c human child

d chick

iii human adult

iv mouse

f young mouse

e kitten

v frog

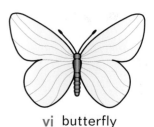

vi butterfly

Challenge

2 Draw the "young" in each empty circle to match the adult.

3 Match the labels to the correct pictures. Write the letters in the boxes.

i elderly woman

ii teenager

iii baby

iv toddler

v adult

vi child

a [ ]   b [ ]   c [ ]   d [ ]   e [ ]   f [ ]

Topic 14: Comparing materials

Get started

A **material** is what an object is made from. Wood, metal, plastic, glass, stone, fabric – these are all materials.

Practice

1 Match the material to its description.

a glass	i hard, strong – good for building houses
b paper	ii light, easy to mould into different shapes – good for making toys
c plastic	iii smooth, transparent (see-through) – good for making windows to let in light and to look through
d foam rubber	iv soft, squashy – good for making mattresses
e stone	v soaks up water, tears easily – good for making tissues

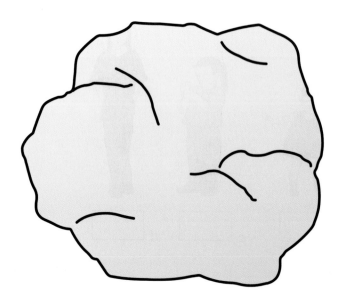

2 Choose the best material for the job. Draw a line to match the material to the object.

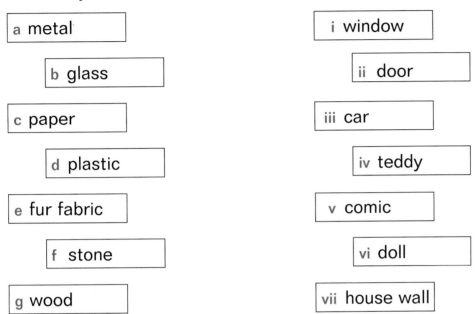

a metal

b glass

c paper

d plastic

e fur fabric

f stone

g wood

i window

ii door

iii car

iv teddy

v comic

vi doll

vii house wall

3 Sort the objects into the correct group. Write the words in the boxes.

glass   brick   plastic ruler   sandpaper   silk fabric   mirror

smooth	rough

Topic 15: Solids, liquids and gases

Materials can be sorted into three groups: **solids**, **liquids** and **gases**.

Liquids flow and change shape to "fit" the container they are held in. Think of the way orange juice can be poured from a carton into a glass. Gases also flow and change shape, but they spread out to completely "fill" a space – even a space as big as a room! Solids do not flow or change shape in the same way.

Practice

1. **Look around the house. Can you see any solids, liquids and gases? Write the names of the things you find in the correct picture below.**

solid   liquid   gas

Challenge

2 **True or false? Put T or F in the boxes.**

a Gas flows and changes shape. . . . . □

b Gas does not flow and change shape. . . . . □

c Oxygen is a gas found in the air we breathe. . . . . □

d Solids flow and change shape to fit containers they are
poured into. . . . . □

e Liquids flow and change shape to fit containers they are
poured into. . . . . □

f Solids do not flow and change shape. . . . . □

g Steam is a gas made when water is boiled. . . . . □

h Gases can spread out to fill any space. . . . . □

3 **Use the clues to fill in the crossword.**

Across

a liquids do, but solids do not

d will not change its shape to fit
a container

Down

b will fit into any container

c will completely fill the container it
is held in

Topic 16: Changes – heating and cooling

Get started

Materials can be changed from one **state** to another by heating or cooling.

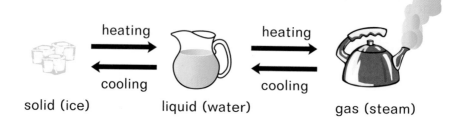

heating →   heating →

← cooling   ← cooling

solid (ice)   liquid (water)   gas (steam)

Practice

1 **How have these materials changed? Write solid, liquid or gas.**

a Chocolate is a solid. When it is heated, it changes into a _____.

b Water is a liquid. When it is heated, it turns into a _____ called "steam".

c Ice is a solid. When it is heated, it changes into a _____.

d When steam (a gas) is cooled, it turns into a _____ called "water".

e Fruit juice is a liquid. When it is cooled in a freezer, it turns into a _____ which we eat as an ice lolly.

Challenge

2 **Some changes can be reversed. This means they can be changed back again. Think of chocolate that has been melted in a pan and then left to go hard again in the fridge.**
Can these changes be reversed? Put a tick for "yes" or a cross for "no".

a Chocolate melting, changing from a solid to a liquid. .... ☐

b Ice melting, changing from a solid to a liquid. .... ☐

c Egg cooking, changing from a liquid to a solid. .... ☐

d Water boiling, changing from a liquid to a gas. .... ☐

e Butter melting, changing from a solid to a liquid. .... ☐

3 **Solid, liquid or gas? Fill in the missing words.**

a Harry is making ice lollies. He mixes fruit juices in a jug. The juices are

_____ .

b His mum Susie decides to have a cup of tea and boils a kettle. Some

of the water changes from a _____ to a _____ as the kettle

boils, filling the kitchen with steam.

c As the steam hits the cold window, it turns back from a _____ to

a _____ .

d Harry puts the lolly mixture into moulds in the freezer. As it cools, it

changes from a _____ to a _____ .

Topic 17: Keeping warm

Some materials are very good at keeping things warm. We call them **thermal insulators**. "Thermal" means "heat".

Do you sleep under a duvet? Duvets are either made of special material called "wadding" or of feathers. Feathers and wadding are both good thermal insulators because they contain lots of air, and the trapped air keeps people warm.

Other materials, such as metals, are good **thermal conductors**. This means that heat passes through them easily. These materials often feel cold if you touch them.

Practice

1 **Which of these materials do you think are good thermal insulators? Put a tick or a cross in the boxes.**

a feathers . . . . ☐   b fur fabric . . . . . . ☐

c air . . . . ☐   d fleece . . . . ☐

e stone . . . . ☐   f metal . . . . ☐

2 **Draw four things that can keep you warm.**

Challenge

3 Complete the sentences in the two boxes, using the words below to fill the gaps.

| heat | insulator | bad | plastic | burn | air | conductor |

a Saucepans are made of metal. Metal is a good thermal _____.

b The _____ moves through the metal and helps the food inside to cook.

c Saucepan handles are often made of _____.

d Plastic is not a good conductor of heat, so you are less likely to _____ your hands!

e Fleece is a good thermal _____. That is why it is used to make jackets.

f Fleece contains lots of trapped _____.

g Air is a _____ conductor of heat, so we are kept warm by the trapped air.

4 If you were designing a cup to keep a drink warm while you were playing in the garden, what would you make it from?
Give a reason for your choice.

| metal | polystyrene | glass | stone |

_____

_____

_____

Topic 18: Sound

Did you know that sound travels in invisible waves through the air? We cannot see them, but we can hear them!

The closer we are to the thing making the noise, the louder it sounds. We hear things as the sound waves enter our ears.

Practice

1 Which of these things are noisy? Which are quiet?
Put a ring around the noisy things.

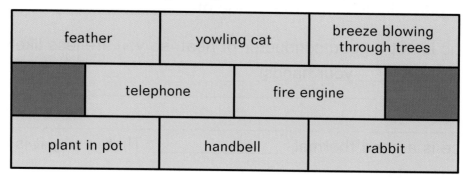

feather	yowling cat	breeze blowing through trees
	telephone	fire engine	
plant in pot	handbell	rabbit

2 Draw three quiet things in the box below.

Challenge

3 **Complete the sentences by circling the correct word.**

a We hear sounds when noise enters our eyes/ears/noses.

b Sound travels through the air in boxes/waves/bubbles.

c We hear the loudest sound when we are close to/far away from/nowhere near the thing making the noise.

d You should never poke things in your ears because you could damage your sight/vision/hearing.

4 **Look at the picture below. Where would the sound from the radio be loudest – at A, at B or at C?**

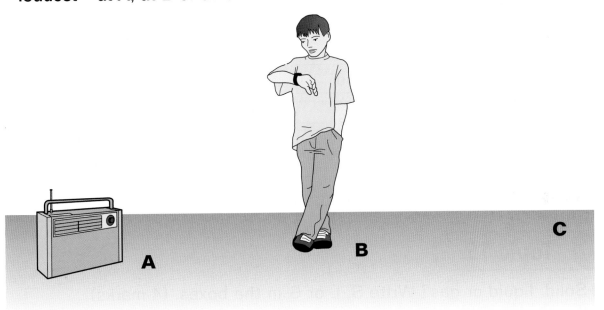

Give a reason for your answer.

_____

_____

_____

_____

Test 3

Topic 13

1 Write these life cycles in order. (3 marks)

a	egg chicken chick	→		→		→	
b	frog frogspawn tadpole	→		→		→	
c	baby woman child	→		→		→	

Topic 14

2 Match the material to the object. (5 marks)

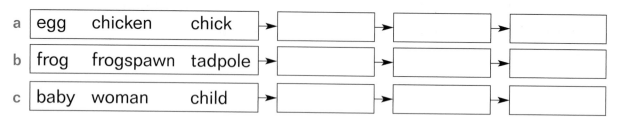

a	chair		i	metal
b	teddy		ii	wood
c	book		iii	glass
d	window		iv	fur fabric
e	pan		v	paper

Topic 15

3 Solid, liquid or gas? Write S, L or G in the boxes. (4 marks)

a stone ☐   b plastic ☐   c water ☐   d steam ☐

e air ☐   f cake ☐   g petrol ☐   h syrup ☐

Topic 16

4 Use the words solid, liquid or gas to complete the sentences. (1 mark)

Robert fills an ice-cube tray with water (a _____) and puts it in the freezer. As the water freezes, it turns into ice (a _____).

Topic 17

5 Which of these materials are good thermal insulators? Circle them. (2 marks)

fleece	wool	metal	glass	feathers

Topic 18

6 True or false? Put T or F in the boxes. (4 marks)

a The closer we are to the thing making the noise, the louder it sounds. . . . . ☐

b We hear sounds when sound waves enter our ears. . . . . ☐

c Sound does not travel through the air. . . . . ☐

d You should never poke things in your ears because you could damage your hearing. . . . . ☐

Mark the test. Remember to fill in your score on page 3.

Write your score out of 19. ☐

Add a bonus point if you scored 15 or more.

TOTAL SCORE FOR TEST 3 ☐

Topic 19: Seasons/Day and night

Get started

Do you know why we have seasons? Or why we have day and night? It is all to do with the movement of the Earth in space. The Earth moves around the Sun once every year. The Earth also spins once every 24 hours. This is one "day" – a day and a night.

The seasons are caused because the Earth is tilted as it moves around the Sun. When the tilt of the north of the Earth is towards the Sun, we have spring and summer in Britain. When the tilt of the north is away from the Sun, we have autumn and winter.

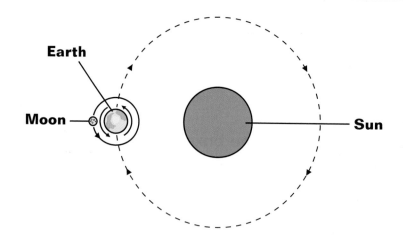

Practice

1 **Fill in the missing words to complete the sentences, using the words in the box below.**

seasons	Earth	Sun	spring	summer	autumn	winter	once

a The _____ moves round the Sun once every year.

b We have _____ because the Earth is tilted as it spins.

c The seasons are called _____, _____, _____ and _____.

d The Earth spins _____ every day.

e As the north tilts towards the _____, we have spring and summer in Britain.

Challenge

2 **Join the two halves of the sentences so that they make sense.**

a The Earth spins once

i causes "night" and "day".

b It is the way the Earth spins that

ii it is "daytime" where you are.

c When the side of the Earth where you are is turned towards the Sun

iii every 24 hours.

d When the side of the Earth where you are is turned away from the Sun

iv it reflects the light from the Sun.

e The Moon "shines" because

v it is "night time" where you are.

3 **True or false? Put T or F in the boxes.**

a The Moon is flat. . . . . ☐

b The Earth is egg-shaped. . . . . ☐

c The Earth is shaped like a ball. . . . . ☐

d The Earth moves round the Sun once every week. . . . . ☐

e The Earth is flat. . . . . ☐

f The Moon is not a source of light, but reflects light from the Sun. . . . . ☐

Topic 20: Forces

Get started

There are many types of forces.

Forces can make things move or stop them moving.

Gravity is a force. It is the force of gravity that makes things fall when they are dropped. The "gravitational pull" of the Earth makes this happen. The gravitational pull of the Earth is strong because the Earth is so big.

Friction is also a force. It slows things down, and can stop things from starting to move. It is friction between our shoes and the floor that stops us slipping over. When it is icy, friction is reduced and we slip and slide.

Practice

1 **Answer these.**

a What is the name of the force that makes things fall when they are dropped? _____

b Which force helps to stop us from slipping over? _____

c Why are we more likely to slip when it is icy? _____

_____

_____

d Why might you slip on a wet floor? _____

_____

e Name two types of forces. _____

f Why do things fall when they are dropped? _____

_____

_____

Challenge

2 **True or false? Put** T **or** F **in the boxes.**

a Friction slows things down. . . . . ☐

b Friction makes things go faster. . . . . ☐

c Gravity makes things fall when they are dropped. . . . . ☐

d Gravity makes things slide about. . . . . ☐

e I would be more likely to slip on a wet floor because there
would be less friction. . . . . ☐

f I would be more likely to slip on a wet floor because there
would be more friction. . . . . ☐

3 **Which thing in each pair would have more friction? Tick the correct
boxes.**

a An ice cube ☐ or a sandpaper block ☐ being pushed along a table

b Someone walking in slippers with rubber soles ☐ or someone walking
in a pair of shoes with shiny leather soles ☐

c A sledge moving on a snow-covered hill ☐ or a sledge moving on a
grassy hill ☐

d A rubber ☐ or a smooth, flat pencil tin ☐ being pushed across a desk

e Someone in socks sliding across a polished floor ☐ or someone in
socks sliding across a rough concrete floor ☐

f A bicycle moving on a flat road ☐ or a bicycle moving on a
gravel path ☐

Topic 21: Floating and sinking

Making sticks or paper boats float is easy. But have you ever wondered how heavy metal ships float? Ships float because they weigh less than the water they push out of the way or **displace**. The air trapped inside the ship makes the ship lighter than the water that it displaces, so the ship floats.

Practice

1 **Which objects will float and which will sink?**
  Fill in the table by ticking "float" or "sink".

object	float	sink
a wooden lolly stick		
b plastic boat		
c metal toy car		
d plastic ball		
e plasticine ball		
f plasticine made into a cup		
g leaf		
h stone		
i polystyrene ball		
j marble		

Challenge

2 **True or false? Put T or F in the boxes.**

a A wooden lolly stick floats in water. . . . . □

b A wooden lolly stick sinks in water. . . . . □

c A marble floats in water. . . . . □

d A plasticine ball floats in water. . . . . □

e A plasticine cup floats in water because the air inside makes
it weigh less than the water it pushes out of the way. . . . . □

f A metal boat could never float. . . . . □

3 **Complete the story using the words in the box below.**

floated	float	displaced	cup	sank	water	air	less

a Ali put a ball of plasticine into some water to see if it would _____.

b The ball _____.

c Then he made the ball into a _____ shape and tried again.

d When he put the cup into the _____, it _____.

e This was because of the _____ inside the cup.

f The air made the cup weigh _____ than the water it pushed
out of the way, or _____.

Topic 22: Light and how we see things

Get started

Light helps us to see things. Light bounces off things and enters our eyes. Light only travels in straight lines – it cannot bend round things.

Shadows are formed when light hits something **opaque** (not see-through) and it cannot pass through.

Practice

1. **Light travels from a source. Look at the wall below. Colour in the things that are sources of light.**

torch	mirror	lamp	shiny pond	
	streetlight	TV screen (on)	candle flame	fire
glass	shiny tin foil	firework	shiny spoon	

Challenge

2 **Reflects light or gives off light? Write R or G in the boxes.**

a candle flame . . . . ☐

b mirror . . . . ☐

c Sun . . . . ☐

d tin foil . . . . ☐

e torch . . . . ☐

f TV screen (on) . . . . ☐

3 **Draw arrows on the picture to show how the boy sees the cat.**

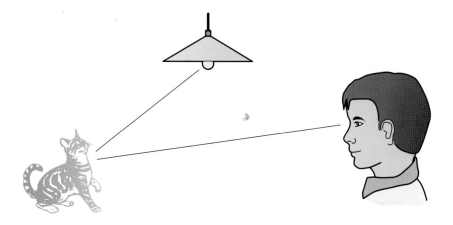

Explain how the boy sees the cat. _____

_____

_____

_____

_____

Topic 23: Magnets

Get started

Magnets attract metals containing iron, such as steel.

The two ends of a magnet are called **poles**. We call them a north pole and a south pole. If you put two poles that are the same together (north + north or south + south), the magnets will push away from each other. We call this **repulsion**. If you put two opposite poles together (north + south), the magnets will be pulled towards each other. We call this **attraction**.

Practice

1 Which objects in the box below will be attracted to a magnet? Circle them.

paper clip   paper

            shell   steel
                                                          needle

                                    plastic
                                      toy
felt tip

            iron   drawing
            nail   pin

                              marble

aluminium   horseshoe
foil sweet
wrapper   gold necklace

Challenge

2 Look at the pairs of bar magnets. Write attract or repel in the boxes to show what will happen.

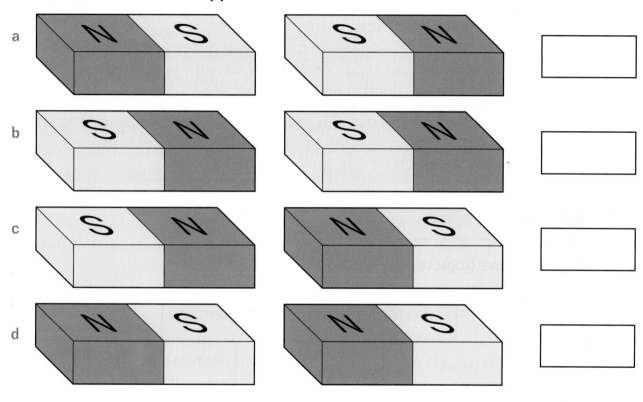

a

b

c

d

3 True or false? Put T or F in the boxes.

a If you put two north poles together, they will repel each other. . . . . . . ☐

b If you put a north and a south pole together, they will be attracted to each other. . . . . ☐

c Plastic is attracted to a magnet. . . . . ☐

d Metals containing iron are attracted to a magnet. . . . . ☐

Topic 24: Electricity and circuits

We use electricity every day: for cooking, lighting, using our computers and so on.

Many things use **mains electricity** – this is the electricity that we get by putting a plug into a wall socket. It can be dangerous. NEVER poke anything into a socket or use plugs and switches with wet hands, because you could get an electric shock.

Battery-powered electricity is used in many toys – this is safer and is the type of electricity you use in circuits at school. Do not take batteries apart. They contain acid which can burn your skin.

Practice

1 **Which of these objects use electricity? Colour them.**

light bulb		fridge		wood fire		street light
	torch		candle		remote-controlled car	
Sun		Moon		coal fire		computer
	mirror		mobile phone		TV	

2 **Which circuit will light the bulb? Remember, electricity must flow round the circuit to make the bulb light.**

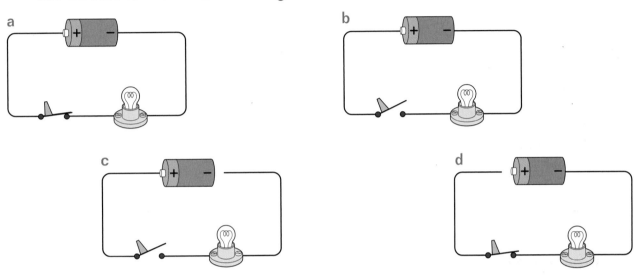

3 **What "jobs" do these circuit components (parts) carry out when they are connected into a circuit? Match the descriptions to the pictures.**

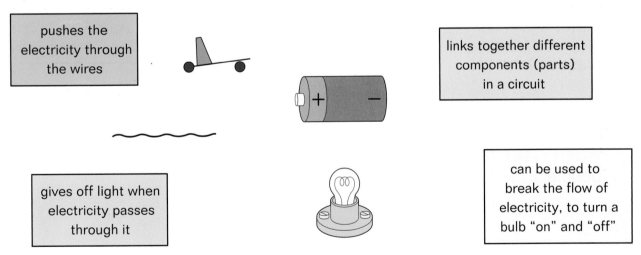

pushes the electricity through the wires

links together different components (parts) in a circuit

gives off light when electricity passes through it

can be used to break the flow of electricity, to turn a bulb "on" and "off"

Test 4

Topic 19

1 What are the four seasons? (2 marks)

_____, _____, _____ and _____.

Topic 20

2 Which force makes things fall to the ground when they are dropped?

(1 mark)_____

3 Which force stops us from slipping over? (1 mark)_____

Topic 21

4 Will these objects float or sink? Write F or S in the boxes. (3 marks)

a empty washing-up bottle ☐

b metal necklace ☐

c plastic plate ☐

d closed empty sandwich box ☐

e plastic dish ☐

f pebble ☐

Topic 22

5 Which of these items are sources of light? Circle them. (3 marks)

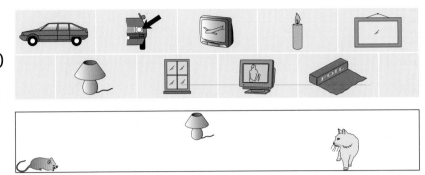

6 Draw arrows to show how the cat sees the mouse. (2 marks)

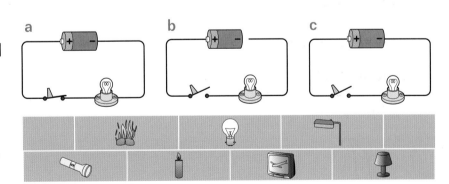

Topic 23

7 True or false? Put T or F in the boxes. (4 marks)

a All metals are attracted to magnets. . . . . □

b Metals containing iron are attracted to magnets . . . . □

c Two north poles would be attracted to each other . . . . □

d Opposite poles attract. . . . . □

Topic 24

8 Which circuit would light the bulb? Tick it. (1 mark)

a   b   c

9 Circle the objects that use electricity. (2 marks)

Mark the test. Now add up all your test scores and put your final score on page 3.

Write your score out of 19.   □

Add a bonus point if you scored 15 or more.   □

TOTAL SCORE FOR TEST 4

Answers

Topic 1: **What do plants need to grow?** (page 4)

1.
a. F
b. T
c. T
d. F
e. T
f. F

2.
a. iii
b. ii
c. iii

3.
a. ii
b. i
c. iii

Topic 2: **Plants from seeds** (page 6)

1.
a. T
b. T
c. T
d. F
e. F

2.
a. germinated
b. seeds
c. temperature
d. trees
e. light

3.
(Variations are possible.)
a. Collect everything I need.
b. Put compost in the pot.
c. Plant the seeds.
d. Water the seeds.

Topic 3: **Parts of a plant** (page 8)

1.

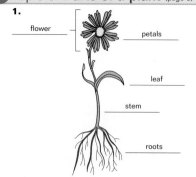

Topic 4: **Sorting** (page 10)

2.
a. roots
b. food
c. pipe
d. petals

3.
a. iii
b. ii
c. iv
d. i

1.
Lives in a pond: frog, great diving beetle
Does not live in a pond: butterfly, grasshopper

2.
Is an insect: grasshopper, ladybird, butterfly
Is not an insect: blackbird
Various answers, e.g. can fly, cannot fly.

3.

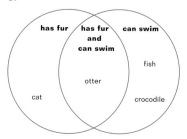

Otters have fur and can swim.

Topic 5: **The seven life processes** (page 12)

1.
a. vi
b. ii
c. i
d. v
e. iii
f. iv

2.
a, b, d, e, g, h, i

3.
Leaf: any living things, plant or animal
Rock: any non-living things such as water, rocks, glass, etc.

Topic 6: **Alive or never alive?** (page 14)

1.
Alive: bird, plant growing in pot, tree, (possibly carrot)
Once alive: dried grass, (possibly carrot)
Never alive: waves, fire, stone

2.
Check that drawings in the first box are of living things.
Can be a variety of answers from animals such as cat, bird, dog or plants like cabbage, dandelion.
Check that drawings in the second box are of non-living things.
Can be a variety of answers such as pebble, metal spoon.

3.
Stone, plastic doll, metal spoon, polystyrene cup, ceramic plate.

Test 1 (page 16)

Topic 1 **1.** It would be yellow and sickly.
2. It would wilt and go brown – and eventually it would die.

Topic 2 **3.** It has started to grow.

Topic 3 **4. a.** iii **b.** ii **c.** i

Topic 4
5. Lives in or near water: tadpole, newt, frog, crab.
Lives on land: cat, badger, horse, butterfly
6. A variety of answers are possible: "can fly" and "cannot fly";
"has 4 legs" and "does not have 4 legs", etc.

Topic 5 **7. a.** F **b.** T **c.** F **d.** T

Topic 6
8. a. N **b.** A **c.** A **d.** A **e.** A **f.** N **g.** N **h.** N **i.** N **j.** N
9. Stone, plastic ruler, china doll, metal spoon

Topic 7: **Habitats** (page 18)

1.
a. i
b. iv
c. ii
d. iii
e. vii
f. viii
g. v
h. vi

2.
a. pond
b. seashore
c. garden
d. woodland
e. hedgerow

3.
A variety of possible answers that could include:
Woodland – owl, squirrel, woodlouse
Pond – newt, toad, frog, diving beetle
Seashore – crab, anemone, starfish
Garden – ladybird, mouse, hedgehog, blackbird

Topic 8: **Caring for the environment** (page 20)

1.
Glass: jam jar, pop bottle
Can: cat food tin, drinks can
Paper: newspaper, comic, magazine

2.
a. iv
b. ii
c. i
d. iii

3.
Any sensible design.

Topic 9: **Senses** (page 22)

1.

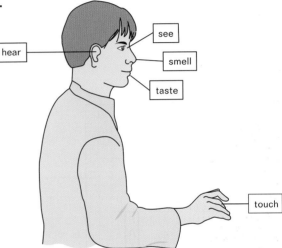

2.
a. nose
b. eyes
c. ears
d. tongue
e. fingers

3.
a. touch
b. smell
c. taste
d. sight
e. hearing

Topic 10: **Teeth** (page 24)

1.
a. chewing
b. clean
c. food
d. Bacteria
e. Plaque
f. decay

2.
a. F
b. T
c. F
d. T
e. F
f. T

3.
There are many acceptable answers. Under the tick – teeth being brushed, visiting the dentist. Under the cross – eating sweets, drinking sugary drinks.

Topic 11: **Food groups** (page 26)

1.
a. banana
b. wholemeal bread
c. pasta
d. milk
e. orange
f. apple juice

2.
Protein – nuts, steak
Fats – cooking oil, butter, nuts
Carbohydrates – pasta, cornflakes

3.

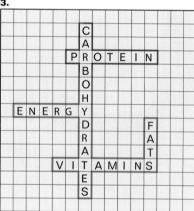

Topic 12: **The heart and exercise** (page 28)

1.
a. heart
b. tubes
c. pulse
d. rises
e. muscles

2.
a. F
b. T
c. F
d. F
e. T
f. F

3.
a. pulse
b. exercise
c. heart
d. veins
e. arteries

4.
A variety of answers are possible including running, playing football, hockey, netball, etc.

Test 2 (page 30)

Topic 7   **1. a.** ii   **b.** iii   **c.** iv   **d.** i

Topic 8   **2. a.** glass lemonade bottle, pickle jar, jam jar
       b. newspaper, magazine, comic
       c. bean tin, lemonade can, cat food tin

Topic 9   **3.** sight, hearing, smell, taste, touch

Topic 10   **4.** To clean away plaque and bits of food; this helps prevent tooth decay.

Topic 11   **5. a.** apple   **b.** fresh orange juice   **c.** carrot sticks

Topic 12   **6. a.** more   **b.** pulse

Topic 13: **Animal life cycles** (page 32)

1.
a. v
b. vi
c. iii
d. ii
e. i
f. iv

2.
Chick (or egg) with chicken, caterpillar with butterfly, tadpole with frog, baby or child with adult human

3.
a. iii   **b.** iv   **c.** vi   **d.** ii   **e.** v   **f.** i

Topic 14: **Comparing materials** (page 34)

1.
a. iii
b. v
c. ii
d. iv
e. i

2.
a. iii
b. i
c. v
d. vi
e. iv
f. vii
g. ii

3.
Smooth: glass, plastic ruler, silk fabric, mirror
Rough: brick, sandpaper

Topic 15: **Solids, liquids and gases** (page 36)

1. A variety of answers are possible including:
Solid: bread, glass, metal
Liquid: water, orange juice
Gas: oxygen, steam, air

2.
a. T
b. F
c. T
d. F
e. T
f. T
g. T
h. T

3.

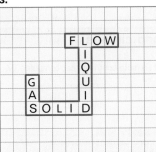

Topic 16: **Changes – heating and cooling** (page 38)

1.
a. liquid
b. gas
c. liquid
d. liquid
e. solid

2.
a. ✓
b. ✓
c. ✗
d. ✓
e. ✓

3.
a. liquid
b. liquid, gas
c. gas, liquid
d. liquid, solid

Topic 17: **Keeping warm** (page 40)

1.
Tick: feathers, fur fabric, air, fleece
Cross: stone, metal

2. Many answers are possible – check they are made from good thermal
insulators.

3.
a. conductor
b. heat
c. plastic
d. burn
e. insulator
f. air
g. bad

4.
Polystyrene, because it is a good thermal insulator so keeps things warm.
Glass, metal and stone do not keep things warm, and metal would get very hot
as you held it – you could burn your hands.

Topic 18: **Sound** (page 42)

1.
Handbell, yowling cat, fire engine, telephone

2.
Any variety of quiet things – a clock ticking, a mouse squeaking, etc.

3.
a. ears
b. waves
c. close to
d. hearing

4.
A, because it is closest to the source of the noise.

Test 3 (page 44)

Topic 13 1. a. egg, chick, chicken
        b. frogspawn, tadpole, frog
        c. baby, child, woman

Topic 14 2. a. ii   **b.** iv   **c.** v   **d.** iii   **e.** i

Topic 15 3. a. S   **b.** S   **c.** L   **d.** G   **e.** G   **f.** S   **g.** L   **h.** L

Topic 16 4. liquid, solid

Topic 17 5. fleece, wool, feathers

Topic 18 6. a. T   **b.** T   **c.** F   **d.** T

Topic 19: **Seasons/Day and night** (page 46)

1.
a. Earth
b. seasons
c. spring, summer, autumn, winter
d. once
e. Sun

2.
a. iii   **b.** i   **c.** ii   **d.** v   **e.** iv

3.
a. F   **b.** F   **c.** T   **d.** F   **e.** F   **f.** T

Topic 20: Forces (page 48)

1.
a. gravity
b. friction
c. There is less friction.
d. There is less friction.
e. gravity and friction (other answers possible)
f. Because of the strong gravitational pull of the Earth.

2.
a. T
b. F
c. T
d. F
e. T
f. F

3.
a. a sandpaper block
b. shoes with rubber soles
c. a sledge moving on a grassy hill
d. a rubber
e. socks sliding across a rough concrete floor
f. bicycle moving on a gravel path

Topic 21: Floating and sinking (page 50)

1.
float: **a b d f g i**
sink: **c e h j**

2.
a. T
b. F
c. F
d. F
e. T
f. F

3.
a. float
b. sank
c. cup
d. water, floated
e. air
f. less, displaced

Topic 22: Light and how we see things (page 52)

1.
Torch, lamp, streetlight, TV screen (on), candle flame, fire, firework

2.
a. G
b. R
c. G
d. R
e. G
f. G

3.

The light from the bulb hits the cat and bounces off the cat into the boy's eyes.

Topic 23: Magnets (page 54)

1.
paper clip, steel needle, iron nail, drawing pin, horseshoe

2.
a. repel   **b.** attract   **c.** repel   **d.** attract

3.
a. T
b. T
c. F
d. T

Topic 24: Electricity and circuits (page 56)

1.
light bulb, fridge, street light, torch, remote-controlled car, computer, TV, mobile phone

2.
Circuit a

3.
Battery – pushes the electricity through the wires.
Wire – links together different components (parts) in a circuit.
Switch – can be used to break the flow of electricity, to turn a bulb "on" and "off".
Bulb – gives off light when electricity passes through it.

Test 4 (page 58)

Topic 19 1. spring, summer, autumn, winter

Topic 20 2. gravity
      3. friction

Topic 21 4. a. F   **b.** S   **c.** F   **d.** F   **e.** F   **f.** S

Topic 22 5. Circled: TV (on), lamp, computer (on), car headlight, candle
      6.

Topic 23 7. a. F   **b.** T   **c.** F   **d.** T

Topic 24 8. a
      9. Torch, light bulb, TV, streetlight, lamp